COOKING WITH SGT. PEREZ

5 Star MREs

By Sgt Perez

ISBN: 979-8-9898191-7-1 (Paperback)

Front cover image by Perez MMG Publishing
Book design by Perez MMG Publishing

Printed in United States of America

First printing edition 2024.

Seerendip Publishing

Introduction

I'm Sergeant Perez, and I LOVE to cook and want to share some of my quick and easy recipes that I have been working on for some time now. In this book, you will find more than 30 easy-to-follow recipes that you can use anytime, anywhere to whip up some tasty grub. They're made with basic ingredients found anywhere in the world, so you won't need to lug around food or bottled water as you move through life—just throw in some fresh produce, stock up on canned goods, and pick up a bag of rice or dried pasta before your next mission!

If you're in the business of tactical operations, or just have a crazy busy life and you find yourself wondering how to make quick, easy meals that don't require hours of preparation, you've come to the right place! In my new cookbook "Quick and Easy Meals for a Tactical Life", you'll find 30+ time-saving recipes that are sure to satisfy your hunger and leave you enough time to plan your next operation... or watch your favorite sitcom! (Because let's face it, life isn't all about work.)

A lot of people these days are living very busy lives. That can mean that they don't always have time to cook themselves something good to eat. That doesn't mean they have to be stuck eating fast food all the time, though. There are some great ways to make healthy, tasty food quickly and easily. I, Sgt. Perez, will show you how with these quick tips! -So go clean out your fridge! You might find a few vegetables or fruits that need to be eaten up soon.

- **Plan:** Look at recipes online, write them down on index cards, or put together meal prep kits in advance so you're ready when hunger strikes.

- **Make it manageable:** Cook just one dish instead of making everything from scratch. Or just make a single pot of soup or chili if you want more than one course but less than four courses.

- **Cook together:** If there's someone else around who is hungry too, maybe the two of you can work together and tackle two dishes at once.

- **Use spices creatively:** They're not just meant to flavor food--spices are also healthy ingredients too! For those times when you don't have much time but want something hearty, delicious, and nutritious - these recipes are for you, Enjoy!

WHAT ARE QUICK MEALS?

In today's world, we're all living busy lives. We have jobs, families and other commitments that pull us in different directions. When time gets tight, it can be tough to find time to cook a healthy meal.

That's where quick meals come in handy! Quick meals are typically pre-packaged meals that you can find at your local grocery store or big box retailer like Costco. They're great because they require little preparation and offer balanced nutrition.

THE BENEFITS OF QUICK MEALS

- Flexible. Order when you want and eat it whenever you like – it's completely flexible as well as quick and easy!
- Easy. Ready meals are so easy!
- Pre-prepared!
- Nutritional Expertise!
- Satisfaction Guaranteed!
- Quality!
- Cost Effectiveness!

Contents

Cheat Sheet for Measurements

Measurement	Spoons/Cups	Fluid Ounces	Milliliters
Pinch/Dash	1/16 teaspoon	-	-
1 teaspoon	-	-	5 ml
1/2 tablespoon	1 1/2 teaspoons	1/4 fl oz	7.5 ml
1 tablespoon	3 teaspoons	1/2 fl oz	15 ml
1 jigger	3 tablespoons	1 1/2 fl oz	45 ml
1/4 cup	4 tablespoons	2 fl oz	60 ml
1/3 cup	5 tablespoons+ 1teaspoon	2 1/2 fl oz	75 ml
1/2 cup	8 tablespoons	4 fl oz	120 ml
2/3 cup	10 tablespoons +2teaspoon	5 fl oz	150 ml
3/4 cup	12 tablespoons	6 fl oz	180 ml
1 cup	16 tablespoons	8 fl oz	240 ml
1 pint	2 cups	16 fl oz	475 ml
1 quart	2 pints or 4 cups	32 fl oz	945 ml
1 gallon	4 quarts or 16 cups	128 fl oz	3.8 liters
1 pound	16 ounces	-	-

Chili with Beans

Ingredients:

- 8 oz. can of tomato sauce
- 16 oz. can red kidney beans, drained and rinsed
- 15 oz. can petite diced tomatoes
- 1 1/2 cups beef broth
- 1/4 teaspoon cayenne pepper, ground
- 1/2 teaspoon black pepper, ground
- 1 1/2 teaspoons salt
- 1 tablespoon garlic powder
- 2 tablespoons tomato paste
- 2 tablespoons granulated sugar
- 2 tablespoons ground cumin
- 2 1/2 tablespoons chili powder
- 1 pound 90% lean ground beef
- 1 medium yellow onion -diced
- 1 tablespoon olive oil

How to Make:

1. In a big soup pot, heat the olive oil over medium-high heat for about two minutes.
2. Mix in the yellow onion and cook, stirring now and then, for around 5 minutes or so.
3. Now move the beef to the large pot, and using a wooden spoon, break the ground beef up.
4. At this point, cook the beef, stirring from time to time, for 6-7 minutes or until the meat is browned.
5. Add in the chili powder, garlic powder, salt, cumin, sugar, tomato paste, pepper, and cayenne if you like.
6. Stir everything until thoroughly combined. Add in the tomatoes along with juice, broth, tomato sauce, and the drained beans, and stir to combine.
7. Bring the liquid mixture to a boil and then set the heat to a low setting.
8. Now carefully simmer the chili, occasionally stirring while not covered for approximately 20 or 25 minutes.
9. Remove the cooking pot from heat, allow the dish to cool down for at least 5 minutes, and then serve.

Calories: 334, Carbs: 34g, Protein: 25g, Fat: 11g

Southwest Style Beef and Black Beans

Prep Time: 15 minutes | Cook Time: 30 minutes | Total Time: 45 minutes | Serves 6

Ingredients:

- 2 (8 oz.) packages of shredded Cheddar cheese
- ½ cup sour cream
- 1 ½ cups water
- 6 oz. can tomato paste
- 15 oz. can black beans, undrained
- 15 oz. can whole kernel corn, drained
- 1 pound ground beef
- 1.25 oz. package taco seasoning mix

Directions:

1. Cook the ground beef in a large pan over medium-high heat, and then discard the extra fat. Stir in the taco seasoning.
2. Turn the heat down to low, cover and allow to simmer for around 10 minutes.
3. Over low heat, mix the corn, tomato paste, beans, and water in a pot.
4. Mix in the sour cream and the seasoned beef, increase the heat then cook for approximately 20 minutes.
5. Transfer the dish into separate serving dishes and top with shredded cheese of your choice.

Calories 635, Fat 39g, Carbs 34g, Protein 39g

Mexican Rice and Bean Bowl

Prep Time: 5 minutes | Cook Time: 20 minutes | Total Time: 25 minutes | Serves 6

Ingredients:

- 1 ½ cups shredded cheese
- ¼ teaspoon garlic powder
- ½ teaspoon ground cumin
- 1 ½ cups salsa
- 1 can of black beans, drained
- 2 cups long grain rice, uncooked
- Salt, to taste
- Sour cream or other salad dressing
- Crushed corn or tortilla chips
- Shredded lettuce

Optional toppings
- Roasted butternut squash
- Fried egg
- Avocado
- Tomatoes
- Green onions
- Peppers
- Corn

Directions:

1. Prepare the rice as per package directions.
2. Whilst rice cooks, heat the salsa, cumin, beans, garlic powder, and salt until evenly heated. Thoroughly stir everything together.
3. Crush the chips and shred the lettuce as needed. Prepare any additional toppings you want to use.
4. Gather 6 bowls and fill each with 1/3 to 1/2 cup salsa and bean mixture, 1 cup rice, and 1/4 cup shredded cheese.
5. Top with chips, sour cream, shredded lettuce, salad dressing, and any of your favorite toppings. Mix and serve!

Calories 482, Protein 17g, Fat 19g, Carbohydrates 66g

Shredded Beef in Barbecue Sauce

Prep Time: 10 minutes | Cook Time: 3 hours | Total Time: 3 hours 10 minutes | Serves 6

Ingredients:

- Ingredients
- 1 bottle BBQ sauce, 28 oz. Bottle
- 1 cup onion, finely chopped
- 2 tablespoons garlic, finely minced
- 3-pound boneless chuck roast, excess fat trimmed
- 2 tablespoons oil
- Pepper, to taste
- Salt, to taste

Directions:

1. In an oven-safe nonstick pot, heat the cooking oil over medium-high heat and then sear all sides of the roast in the pan.
2. Next, sauté the garlic and onion for around 2 minutes or until fragrant.
3. Mix in the barbecue sauce, salt, and pepper, then cook until the roast is completely coated.
4. Cook for 3 hours, covered, at 325°F, while mixing everything after about 1 1/2 hours.
5. Move the dish to a stovetop and cook until the liquid is reduced to your preferred consistency.
6. Using two forks, shred the beef and serve the sandwiches with the pulled beef.
7. 7. Consider storing any leftovers for up to 3 days in the refrigerator.

Calories: 593, Carbs: 34g, Protein: 44g, Fat: 31g

Beef Taco Filling

Prep Time: 15 minutes | Cook Time: 25 minutes | Total Time: 40 minutes | Serves 8-12

Ingredients:

- 15 oz. can of tomato sauce
- 1/4 teaspoon red pepper flakes, optional
- 1/2 teaspoon onion salt
- 1/2 teaspoon dried oregano
- 1/2 teaspoon ground coriander
- 2 teaspoons ground cumin
- 2 tablespoons chili powder
- 1 seeded and finely diced jalapeno
- 3-4 cloves garlic - minced
- 1 small onion, diced
- 2 pounds ground beef
- Salt, to taste
- Pepper, to taste

Directions:

1. Cook ground meat with garlic, onion, and jalapeño in a large pan over medium heat, and break the meat as you cook.
2. Cook until the meat is cooked through, or for about 6-8 minutes, and then drain any excess fat.
3. Mix in all of the spices, as well as pepper and salt to taste. Cook for 1 or 2 more minutes.
4. Add the tomato sauce and mix well. Simmer for 15-20 minutes, covered. If necessary, season with a little pepper and salt.
5. Serve with tortillas, taco shells, and your preferred taco toppings.

Calories 179 kcal, Protein 20.85 g, Fat 8.88g, Carbohydrates: 3.29 g

Beef Strips in Tomato Sauce

Prep Time: 15 minutes | Cook Time: 15 minutes | Total Time: 30 minutes |
Serves 2-4

Ingredients:

- 2 cups of pasta sauce
- 1 large sweet onion, chopped
- Salt & pepper to taste
- 2 strip steaks
- 1 tablespoon olive or avocado oil
- ½ cup Argiano Rosso Toscana

Directions:

1. Over medium-high heat, heat a sturdy, oven-safe saute pan. Once hot, add in the oil.

2. Dry the steaks thoroughly with paper towels and season both sides of the steak liberally with pepper and salt.

3. Sear the steaks for 30 seconds on each side in the hot pan.

4. Broil the steak for 2 minutes in the oven. Flip and then broil again for another 2 minutes. You should now have a steak that is medium-rare steak. Remove the steak from the pan then set aside 1 tablespoon of the pan drippings and then clean the pan.

5. Return the drippings to the cooking pan, then add the chopped onions and sauté the ingredients over medium heat settings. Cook everything until translucent.

6. Pour in the wine and sauce, and then bring to a simmer. Cook until the wine has been reduced and the sauce has thickened.

7. Return the steaks to the pan, lower the heat to low, and let the steaks warm up in the sauce for approximately 2 minutes. This will yield a medium-rare steak.

8. Let the steak rest for 3 minutes, and then serve it with the sauce on top.

Calories 253 kcal, Protein 27.33g, Fat 8.38g, Carbohydrates 17.72g

Beef Stew

Prep Time: 10 minutes | Cook Time: 1 hr 15 min | Total Time: 1 hr 25 minutes | Serves 4

Ingredients:

- Salt and pepper, to taste
- 4 bay leaves
- 2 sprigs of thyme, whole
- 1 carrot, peeled and roughly chopped
- 2 stalks of celery, roughly chopped
- 1 onion, diced
- 4 slices of bacon, diced
- 1 pound of beef stew meat (cubes)
- 2 cups of cold water
- 2 tablespoons of avocado oil to cook with

Directions:

1. Put the avocado oil in a big pot and then cook the bacon and red meat over high heat.
2. Then add in the onion and allow it to cook for a couple of minutes. Add the water and bring it to a boil.
3. Add in the bay leaves, thyme, carrot, and celery, then season gently with salt and pepper. Bring to a simmer with the lid closed until the beef is soft or for about 60 minutes.
4. Discard the thyme stalks and bay leaves—season with extra pepper and salt to taste.
5. You can garnish with the remaining thyme leaves if you like.

Calories 505, Fat 44g, Carbs 4g, Protein 22g

Beef Goulash

Prep Time: 15 minutes | Cook Time: 30 minutes | Total Time: 35 minutes | Serves 10

Ingredients:

- 1 cup cheddar cheese, shredded
- 2 cups macaroni noodles, uncooked
- 3 bay leaves
- 2 tablespoons Italian Seasoning
- 2 teaspoons seasoned salt
- 3 tablespoons Worcestershire Sauce
- 3 cups beef broth
- 2 15 oz. cans petite diced tomatoes
- 2 15 oz. cans tomato sauce
- 3 teaspoons garlic, minced
- 2 lbs. ground beef, lean
- 1 green bell pepper, diced
- 1 cup onion, diced
- 1 tablespoon olive oil

Directions:

1. Heat the olive oil in a large saucepan, over medium-high heat
2. Add in the ground beef, onion, and bell pepper, and then cook until the meat is no longer pink.
3. Drain any extra fat and place the saucepan on the stovetop. Stir in the garlic for approximately 30 seconds or until fragrant.
4. Mix in the beef broth, Worcestershire sauce, tomato sauce, chopped tomatoes, bay leaves, seasoned salt, Italian seasoning, and dry macaroni noodles.
5. Stir for a moment, and then bring the mixture to a boil. Reduce the heat to low and simmer for about 20 minutes until the pasta is cooked.
6. Discard the bay leaves, mix in the cheese and serve.
7. Calories 328, Protein 28g, Fat 12g, Carbohydrates 25g

Beef Ravioli

Prep Time: 20 minutes | Cook Time: 25 minutes | Total Time: 45 minutes | Serves 6

Ingredients:

Filling
- 1 egg
- 1/2 teaspoon salt
- 2 tablespoons grated Parmesan cheese
- 1/4 cup minced fresh parsley
- 1 clove garlic, minced
- 1 small onion, minced
- 1/2 pound ground beef

Ravioli Dough
- 1 teaspoon salt
- 1 tablespoon olive or salad oil
- 1/4 cup water
- 2 eggs
- 2 1/4 cups all-purpose flour

Marinara Sauce
- 6 ounce can tomato paste
- 16 ounce can diced tomatoes, undrained
- 1 teaspoon salt
- 2 teaspoons dried basil
- 1 tablespoon sugar
- 1 clove garlic, minced
- 1 small onion, chopped
- 2 tablespoons olive or salad oil

Directions:

1. For the filling: Heat a pan over medium heat. Add in the onion, ground meat, and garlic.
2. Cook while stirring until the onions are soft and the meat is cooked through. Remove any excess oil.
3. Turn off the heat and add the cheese, parsley, and salt. Combine well, then add the egg.
4. Put the meat and onion mixture in a container then close it and keep refrigerated while you complete the remaining portion of the recipe.
5. For the dough: in a large mixing bowl, put the flour and then add in the water, oil, eggs, and salt.
6. Stir in the flour until you have a firm dough. Place the dough on a well-floured surface and knead until the dough is soft and stretchy.
7. Wrap the dough with cling film and allow it to set for 30 minutes or so.

8. Cut the dough into four evenly sized portions. Roll out the portions to a 12x8-inch rectangle on a floured board.

9. With a knife, gently score a pattern of 24 2-inch squares. Top the center of each square with a spoonful of the meat filling.

10. Roll out another dough portion into a 12x8-inch rectangle. Put gently on top of the first layer of dough.

11. To seal, squeeze the dough down all around the filling and the corners. Divide the dough into squares gently over each mound of filling.

12. Close the edges of each square piece as necessary. Put the ravioli in a single layer on a kitchen towel and set aside for half an hour to dry.

13. Continue the process with the rest of the dough and filling.

14. Make the marinara sauce while the ravioli is drying.

15. In a saucepan over medium heat, heat the oil until it's hot. Cook the garlic and onions until the onion is tender.

16. Mix in the basil, tomatoes, sugar, salt, and tomato paste in the saucepan. Bring the mixture to a boil, and then lower the heat.

17. Cook while covered, for approximately 20 minutes making sure you stir periodically.

18. To prepare the ravioli: over high heat, bring a large pot of salted water to a boil.

19. Add in and cook the ravioli, tossing around to keep the dough pieces from clinging. Bring the ravioli to a boil and then lower it to a good simmer.

20. Cook until the pasta is done or for around 5 minutes then drain.

21. Put the cooked ravioli in separate serving dishes. Serve with the marinara sauce on top. If you would like, you can top with parmesan cheese and enjoy.

Calories 678, Carbs 75g, Protein 26g, Fat 31g,

Meatballs in Marinara Sauce

Prep Time: 20 minutes | Cook Time: 30 minutes | Total Time: 50 minutes | Serves 4

Ingredients:

Meatballs
- 2 eggs, beaten
- 1/4 cup milk
- 1/2 teaspoon black pepper, freshly ground
- 1 teaspoon salt
- 1 teaspoon Italian seasoning
- 1 clove garlic, minced
- 2 teaspoons dried parsley
- 1/4 cup Parmesan cheese
- 1/2 cup Italian-flavored panko crumbs
- 1 lb. ground beef

Marinara Sauce
- 12 torn basil leaves
- 1 tablespoon granulated sugar
- 1/4 teaspoon red pepper flakes
- 1 teaspoon black pepper, freshly ground
- 1 teaspoon kosher salt
- 2 teaspoons Italian seasoning
- 1 28 oz. can San Marzano-style crushed tomatoes
- 1 28-oz. can of chopped tomatoes in puree, San Marzano style
- 6 cloves garlic, minced
- 3/4 cup yellow onion, chopped
- 1/4 cup olive oil

Directions:

1. To make the meatballs, first, preheat your oven to 350°F. Then using parchment paper, line a large baking sheet and set the sheet aside.

2. Now mix all meatball ingredients in a large mixing bowl and then form balls using a small 1 1/2-inch scoop.

3. Bake the meatballs on the prepared baking sheet for approximately 20 minutes, flipping halfway through. Remove from oven and finish the cooking by adding in marinara sauce.

4. To prepare the marinara sauce, heat olive oil in a large saucepan over medium-high heat.

5. Then add the chopped onion and cook for about 3-4 minutes, or until the onion is translucent while stirring continuously.

6. Add in the garlic and cook for one more minute while stirring. Stir in the rest of the ingredients, excluding the basil leaves, until well incorporated.

7. Simmer for 30 minutes on low heat.

8. Then add the meatballs and the torn basil leaves and cook the meatballs until warmed through.

Calories: 561, Carbs: 20g, Protein: 28g, Fat: 41g

Spaghetti with Beef and Sauce

Prep Time: 25 minutes | **Cook Time:** 3 hours | **Total Time:** 3 Hours 25 minutes | Serves 10

Ingredients:

- 1 pound dried spaghetti noodles
- 1 teaspoon black pepper, freshly ground
- 1 teaspoon kosher salt
- 1 teaspoon oregano
- 1 teaspoon basil
- 1/4 cup chopped fresh or 4 teaspoons dried parsley
- 2 tablespoons sugar
- 2 bay leaves
- 5-6 whole cloves
- 1 15- ounce can of beef broth
- 1 cup red wine
- 2 7- ounce cans of sliced mushrooms
- 1 6- ounce can of tomato paste
- 1 29- ounce can of tomato sauce
- 1 29- ounce can of diced tomatoes
- 4 garlic cloves minced or pressed
- 4 stalks of celery chopped
- 1 yellow onion chopped
- 1 pound 85% lean ground beef
- Grated Parmesan cheese

Directions:

1. Sauté the ground beef in a large heavy-bottomed stock pot over medium-high heat until golden brown, or for approximately 5-7 minutes, stirring now and again.
2. Then, discard the rendered fat and return the meat to the cooking pot.
3. Now add in garlic, celery, and chopped onion and cook for additional 5-7 minutes, or until the vegetables become soft.
4. Stir in the remaining ingredients (besides the Parmesan and spaghetti noodles) and bring to a boil.
5. Lower the heat to medium-low, stir for a few seconds, and cook while covered for at least three hours, stirring once in a while.
6. Cook the spaghetti in salted water based on the package directions. Then drain the spaghetti and incorporate it into the spaghetti sauce.

7. If you like it, top it with ground or grated Parmesan cheese along with freshly chopped parsley.

8. Know that the meat sauce can be kept in the fridge for up to a whole week or, if frozen, can last up to 3 months inside a gallon ziplock bag.

Calories: 365, Carbs: 52g, Protein: 18g, Fat: 8g

Chili and Macaroni

Prep Time: 10 minutes | Cook Time: 20 minutes | Total Time: 30 minutes | Serves 6

Ingredients:

- ½ teaspoon ground cumin
- 1 ½ tablespoon chili powder
- 6-ounce can of tomato paste
- 8-ounce can of tomato sauce
- 14.5 ounce can of diced tomatoes undrained
- 15-ounce can of kidney beans drained
- 2 cloves garlic minced
- 1 small onion diced
- 1 pound ground beef
- 1 cup uncooked macaroni
- 1 cup cheddar cheese for topping, shredded
- Salt and pepper, to taste

Directions:

1. Cook and simmer the macaroni until it is tender. Meanwhile, brown the ground beef with the onion.
2. Once the beef has browned and the onion is soft, add the garlic during the last few minutes of cooking (to avoid burning).
3. Discard any excess grease from the ground beef and return it to the cooking pot. Wait for the macaroni to be fully cooked, and then drain it.
4. Now stir the cooked macaroni and the rest of the ingredients into the beef mixture except the cheddar cheese.
5. Bring to a boil, stir for a few seconds and then reduce to low heat. Now cover and simmer for approximately 15-20 minutes.
6. At this point, give it a taste test and consider seasoning it with a pinch of salt.
7. Finally, serve with shredded cheese sprinkled on top of each serving.

Calories: 371, Carbs: 21g, Protein: 21g, Fat: 22g

Elbow Macaroni

Prep Time: 10 minutes | Cook Time: 10 minutes | Total Time: 20 minutes | Serves 10

Ingredients:

- 2 green onions, chopped
- 1½ tablespoons of Dijon mustard
- 1½ tablespoons of apple cider vinegar
- 1½ tablespoons of sugar
- ¼ cup of sour cream
- 1 cup of mayo
- 1 cup of shredded carrots
- 2 stalks of celery, finely chopped
- 1 red pepper, diced
- 1 1-pound box of elbow macaroni, cooked
- 1 tablespoon parsley, chopped

Directions:

1. Boil pasta according to package directions in a large pot. It is best to undercook it a little, so that it doesn't become soggy once you add the dressing. Drain, but do not rinse the cooked pasta.
2. Toss the pasta in a large mixing bowl with olive oil to keep it from sticking together.
3. Add in the rest of the ingredients except the ingredients for the dressing.
4. In a small mixing bowl, combine the vinegar, sour cream, sugar, mustard, mayonnaise, and parsley to prepare the salad dressing.
5. Pour the dressing over the salad quite generously.
6. Mix then chill the elbow salad for at least two to six hours before serving.

Calories 278 kcal, Protein 7.08 g, Fat 10.89 g, Carbohydrates 38.24 g

Mexican Style Chicken Stew

Prep Time: 15 minutes | **Cook Time:** 4-5 hours | **Total Time:** 4hours 15 minutes | **Serves** 9

Ingredients:

- 1 (1-ounce) can whole kernel corn
- 8-ounce can tomato sauce
- 1.25-ounce package taco seasoning mix
- 4-ounce can diced green chilies
- 16-ounce jar mild salsa
- 1/2 teaspoon salt
- 3 medium russet potatoes, diced into small pieces
- 6 (1½-inch) pieces boneless, skinless chicken thigh fillets
- Warm flour tortillas, optional

Directions:

1. In a crockpot, combine potatoes, tomato sauce, taco seasoning mix, salt, salsa, chicken thighs, green chilies, and corn.
2. Cook on high for 4 to 5 hours, stirring from time to time.
3. Serve the chicken stew with warm flour tortillas.

Calories 250, Protein 25grams

Chicken Burrito Bowl

Prep Time: 5 minutes | Cook Time: 20 minutes | Total Time: 25 minutes | Serves 4

Ingredients:

- ¼ cup shredded cheddar cheese
- ¼ cup sour cream
- 1 avocado sliced
- 2 cups chopped romaine lettuce
- 1 cup rice - boiled
- 1 cup black beans, canned
- 1 cup canned corn
- 1/2 teaspoon black pepper
- 1/2 teaspoon salt
- 1/2 teaspoon ground chili pepper
- 1 teaspoon cumin
- 1 teaspoon paprika
- 2 tablespoons extra virgin olive oil
- 2 chicken breasts

For salsa:

- Juice of 2 limes
- 2 tablespoons white vinegar
- ½ onion chopped
- ½ tomato chopped
- 1 tablespoon finely chopped cilantro
- Pinch of salt

Directions:

1. Chop the chicken breast into easy-to-bite pieces.
2. Add the chunks of chicken breast to a medium bowl along with the ground red pepper flakes, cumin, olive oil, paprika, salt, and black pepper.
3. Mix vigorously until the chicken is well covered with the oil and spices.
4. Preheat a nonstick skillet over medium heat. Cook the chicken in the hot pan until thoroughly cooked through or for 7-8 minutes on each side. Set aside the cooked chicken.
5. Now cook rice per package directions.
6. Combine rice, beans, chopped lettuce, corn, and cooked chicken in a large mixing dish.
7. On top, layer salsa, sour cream, chopped avocado, and cheese.
8. To prepare the salsa: Cut the tomato, cilantro, and onion finely and put in a bowl.
9. 9. Add in the lime juice, vinegar, and salt. Mix everything up until thoroughly incorporated.

Calories 618, fat 24g, carbs 67g, protein 37g

Chicken, Egg Noodles, and Vegetables in Sauce

Prep Time: 10 minutes | **Cook Time:** 15 minutes | **Total Time:** 25 minutes | **Serves** 4

Ingredients:

- 1/4 cup sliced dark green onion tops
- 2 teaspoons cornstarch
- 1 tablespoon sesame oil
- 2 tablespoons soy sauce
- 2 tablespoons hoisin sauce
- 1/4 cup chicken broth
- 1/2 teaspoon ginger minced
- 1 teaspoon garlic - minced
- 1/2 cup thinly sliced red bell pepper
- 1/4 cup celery, thinly sliced
- 1/2 cup shredded or julienned carrots
- 3/4 cup shiitake mushrooms stems removed, thinly sliced
- 10 ounces fresh egg noodles pre-cooked
- 3/4 pound boneless, thinly sliced skinless chicken breasts
- 1 tablespoon vegetable oil
- Pepper, to taste
- Salt

Directions:

1. In a large skillet over medium-high heat, heat the vegetable oil.
2. Add the chicken breasts to the pan and then season them with a bit of salt and pepper. Cook until golden brown, which is about 3-4 minutes per side.
3. Remove the chicken from the pan, then add mushrooms, red bell pepper, carrots, and celery to the pan.
4. Cook for 4-5 minutes or until the ingredients are barely softened.
5. Mix in the ginger and garlic, and then cook for about 30 seconds.
6. Add the noodles and the chicken to the pan, then toss to mix everything together.
7. Whisk together the hoisin sauce, chicken broth, sesame oil, cornstarch, and soy sauce in a small bowl.
8. Pour the sauce into a pan, then bring the sauce to a simmer in a saucepan. Cook until the sauce thickens or for around 1 minute or so. Add in the green onions, then serve.

Calories: 336, Carbs: 37g, Protein: 25g, Fat: 11g

Cabanossi Cheese Pizza Slice

Prep Time: 10 minutes | **Cook Time:** 15 minutes | **Total Time:** 25 minutes | **Serves** 8

Ingredients:

- 12 Pitted kalamata olives
- 100g Cabanossi / mild salami, thinly sliced
- 1/2 capsicum, finely chopped
- 4 tablespoons Store-bought pizza sauce
- 60g butter, melted
- 1/2 cup milk
- 1 egg
- 1 teaspoon dried oregano
- 1/2 cup grated cheese, plus $\frac{1}{3}$ cup extra
- 1/4 teaspoon Salt
- 1/2 teaspoon Baking powder
- 1 cup Self-rising flour

Directions:

1. Heat the oven to 200°C. Line a 30 x 20cm slice pan with parchment paper, stretching it over the sides.
2. In a large bowl, sift together the baking powder, flour, and salt. Add in half a cup of preferred cheese, plus oregano.
3. In the center of the cheese and flour mixture, make a well. Then in a small jug, whisk the egg, butter, and milk.
4. Pour the combination directly into the flour and cheese mixture. Fold the contents together slowly with a big spoon until just blended.
5. Now distribute into the prepared baking dish. Add pizza sauce to the mixture's surface.
6. Add additional cheese, cabanossi, olives, and sliced capsicum on top. Cook until golden or for 20 to 25 minutes.
7. Once done, let the pizza rest for 5 minutes in the pan before transferring it to a wire rack to cool. To serve, cut into slices.
8. You can also add any of your preferred toppings, such as pineapple, tomatoes, onions, ham, or artichokes.

Calories 216, Protein 10.2g, Fat 13.39g, Carbohydrates 13.36g

Cheese Tortellini

Prep Time: 5 minutes | Cook Time: 25 minutes | Total Time: 30 minutes | Serves 6-8

Ingredients:

Fresh Pasta
- 1/2 teaspoon kosher salt
- 1 teaspoon olive oil
- 3 tablespoons water
- 2 large eggs
- 3 cups all-purpose flour

Tortellini
- 1 large egg, beaten with 1/2 teaspoon water
- 1 pinch nutmeg, freshly grated
- 1/4 teaspoon black pepper, freshly ground
- 1 large egg
- 2 tablespoons spinach, chopped
- 1/4 cup Parmesan cheese, grated
- 1/2 cup ricotta cheese

Directions:

1. To prepare fresh pasta by hand, form a well with the flour on a clean surface.

2. Combine the cooking oil, eggs, water, and salt in a measuring cup.

3. Transfer the wet mixture gently into the flour and mix with 2 fingers until completely integrated; without forcing the dough to incorporate all the flour.

4. To make the fresh pasta using a food processor: Combine the flour and salt in a food processor bowl and pulse 2 to 3 times.

5. Whisk the eggs, oil, and water in a liquid measuring cup. Pour this liquid into the machine in a steady stream while pulsing it.

6. Then continue pulsing it until the dough starts to pull away from the edges of the food processor bowl.

7. If you're using a pasta machine for rolling out your dough, shape it into a disk and wrap it in plastic wrap now.

8. Refrigerate for 1 hour to let the flavors blend. If rolling manually by hand, knead the dough for approximately 8 to 10 minutes on a floured work surface.

9. Tortellini preparation: In a medium mixing bowl, mix egg, spinach, all the cheeses, black pepper, and nutmeg. Put the mixture aside.

10. You may roll out tortellini dough by machine or by hand. Cut the dough into 3- or 4-inch circles using a round cookie cutter.

11. Top each round with a quarter teaspoon of the filling. To seal, apply egg wash to the round's bottom half and fold it over.

12. To create a tortellini, fold the dough around your finger and turn down the edge.

13. In a large saucepan, bring 2 quarts of salted water to a boil, then add the prepared tortellini dough in stages.

14. Cook for approximately 3 to 5 minutes or until they float to the surface.

15. Transfer the tortellini to a sieve to drain, and then toss them with the sauce of choice.

Maple Pork Sausage Patty

Prep Time: 15 minutes | **Cook Time:** 10 minutes | **Total Time:** 25 minutes | **Serves** 8

Ingredients:

- 1 pound ground pork
- 1/4 teaspoon cayenne pepper
- 1/2 teaspoon ground nutmeg
- 1/2 teaspoon poultry seasoning
- 1/2 teaspoon dried thyme
- 1/2 teaspoon rubbed sage
- 1/2 teaspoon onion powder
- 1/2 teaspoon salt
- 1 tablespoon maple syrup
- 1 to 2 teaspoons liquid smoke, optional

Directions:

1. Mix the spices, maple syrup, salt, and, if you like liquid smoke in a large mixing bowl.
2. Mix in the pork gently but firmly. Use the mixture to form eight 2-1/2-inch patties. Put it in the fridge for at least 1 hour while covered.
3. Cook patties in a large pan sprayed with cooking spray over medium heat for about 4-6 minutes per side or until a thermometer reads 160°.

Calories, Fat 8g, Carbs 2g, Protein 10g

Jalapeno Pepper Jack Beef Burgers

Prep Time: 10 minutes | Cook Time: 10 minutes | Total Time: 20 minutes | Serves 4

Ingredients:

- Ingredients
- 1 tablespoon Worcestershire sauce
- 1 8 oz. block pepper jack cheese
- 2 jalapenos removed and minced seeds
- 1 1/2 pounds ground beef
- Pepper
- Kosher salt
- Optional
- Burger buns
- Ketchup, toppings
- Lettuce
- Tomato

Directions:

1. Cut the jack cheese in half; cut one half into small cubes, and then reserve the remaining half.
2. Mix the jack cheese cubes in a mixing bowl with kosher salt, Worcestershire sauce, ground beef, and pepper.
3. Mix the beef and sauce mixture and then form four burger patties.
4. Heat the grill to medium-high and grill the patties for 4 to 5 minutes per side.
5. Cut the remaining pepper jack cheese into slices. Put them on the burgers at the last minute of cooking.
6. Serve the patties on the buns with desired toppings such as lettuce, onion, tomato and ketchup.

Calories 589, Protein 59.66, Fat 36.17, Carbohydrates 3.47

Italian Sausage with Peppers and Onions

Prep Time: 15 minutes | Cook Time: 30 minutes | Total Time: 45 minutes | Serves 4-6

Ingredients:

- ¼ cup white wine
- 1 teaspoon dried oregano
- 1 teaspoon dried basil
- 1 medium green bell pepper, sliced
- 1 large red bell pepper, sliced
- 4 cloves garlic, minced
- ½ medium red onion, sliced
- 1 medium yellow onion, sliced
- 2 tablespoons butter
- 6 (4 ounce) links sweet Italian sausage

Directions:

1. Cook Italian sausage in a large pan over medium heat for 5 to 7 minutes or until brown on both sides. Remove the sausage from the skillet and cut it into slices.
2. In the same skillet, melt the butter. Mix in the garlic and onions and then cook for 2 to 3 minutes.
3. Season with basil and oregano, and add bell peppers. Pour in the 1/4 cup wine and cook while stirring for about 5 to 7 minutes or until the onions and pepper are soft.
4. Put the semi-cooked sausage pieces in the pan, lower the heat, cover, and cook on low heat until the sausage is well cooked, or for 15 minutes. If necessary, add extra wine.

Calories 546, Protein 54.7g, Fat 32g, Carbohydrates 9g

Lemon Pepper Tuna

Prep Time: 10 minutes | Cook Time: 10 minutes | Total Time: 20 minutes | Serves 4

Ingredients:

- 2 cloves garlic minced
- 1 tablespoon extra-virgin olive oil
- 1 tablespoon butter, unsalted
- 2 tablespoons fresh lemon juice
- 2 tablespoons preferred lemon pepper seasoning
- 2 ½ pounds Yellowfin Tuna Fillets

Directions:

1. First, remove the fillets from the fridge. Rinse them in the sink under cold running water.
2. Put the fish on a dish and blot them dry with a clean paper towel.
3. Squeeze a little lemon juice over each tuna steak and liberally season both sides of the steak with lemon pepper seasoning.
4. In a cast iron pan, heat 1 tablespoon of extra virgin olive oil along with 1 tablespoon butter.
5. When the butter and olive oil are heated, add around two pieces of crushed garlic. Cook until the garlic is fragrant but do not let it brown.
6. Carefully coat the tuna steaks with the garlic and then flip them over to cook the other side. Sear the fish for about 4 minutes each side over medium-high heat.
7. Remove the steaks from the cooking pan and set aside for a few minutes to rest.
8. Cut the tuna steaks into four parts, drizzle with more lemon juice if needed, and then serve.

THANK YOU & ENJOY!

No matter how busy your life is, you can always find time to cook a delicious and nutritious meal. With a little planning and the right ingredients, you can make a meal that will not only taste good but will also help you stay healthy and fit. We hope that these recipes have inspired you to get in the kitchen and start cooking for yourself. If you're looking for some quick and easy meal ideas that are perfect for a busy, tactical lifestyle, then cooking with Sgt. Perez is the way to go. My recipes are simple but delicious, and they can be easily tailored to your own personal preferences. Plus, my tips on food storage and preparation will help you save time and hassle in the kitchen.

In conclusion, the book is a great way to improve your health and is a great way to make quick meals that are nutritious and delicious. With a little bit of planning, you can make sure that you always have something healthy and tasty to eat, no matter how busy your life gets.

Thanks for reading!

Appendix

The last thing I'm going to leave you with is a cooking conversion chart. This is to help you out if you need to convert measurements, or anything of the like so that you can enjoy the recipes from anywhere in the world.

Dry Weights

Ounces	Tablespoons	Cups	Grams	Pounds
½ ounce	1 tablespoon	1/16 cup	15 grams	---
1 ounce	2 tablespoons	1/8 cup	28 grams	---
2 ounces	4 tablespoons	¼ cup	57 grams	---
3 ounces	6 tablespoons	1/3 cup	85 grams	---
4 ounces	8 tablespoons	½ cup	115 grams	¼ pound
8 ounces	16 tablespoons	1 cup	227 grams	½ pound
12 ounces	24 tablespoons	1 ½ cups	340 grams	¾ pound
16 ounces	32 tablespoons	2 cups	455 grams	1 pound

Oven Temp

Celcius	240	230	220	200	190	180	170	150	140	120
Farenheit	475	450	425	400	375	350	325	300	275	250

Liquid Conversions

- "One gallon = 4 quarts, 8 pints, 16 cups, 128 fluid ounces, 3.8 liters

- One quart = 2 pints, 4 cups, 32 fluid ounces, 946 milliliters

- One pint = 2 cups, 16 fluid ounces, 470 milliliters

- One cup = 16 tablespoons, 8 fluid ounces, 240 milliliters

- ¼ cup = 4 tablespoons, 2 fluid ounces, 12 teaspoons, 60 milliliters"

Liquid Volumes

Ounces	Teaspoons	Tablespoons	Milliliters	Cups	Pints	Quarts
1	6	2	30	1/8	--	--
2	12	4	60	¼	--	--
2 2/3	16	5	80	1/3	--	--
4	24	8	120	½	--	--
5 1/3	32	11	160	2/3	--	--
6	36	12	177	¾	--	--
8	48	16	240	1	½	¼
16	96	32	470	2	1	½
32	192	64	950	4	2	1

- 1 tsp = 5mL
- 1 tbsp = 15 mL
- Dash = 1/16 tsp
- Pinch = 1/8 tsp

Conclusion

You've reached the end of *Cooking With Sgt Perez*. I hope that you enjoy all of the recipes, and find them easy and enjoyable to make. I hope that the cookbook is something that you use over and over again, and enjoy the recipes. Lastly, I would like to ask that if you have found the book helpful in any way, a positive review on Amazon or with Barnes & Noble is always helpful.

BUT WAIT

THERE'S MORE

I WANTED TO ALSO
THROW IN A FEW
RECIPES FROM MY
OTHER BOOKS

CHECK OUT

THESE OTHER COOKBOOKS FROM SGT PEREZ

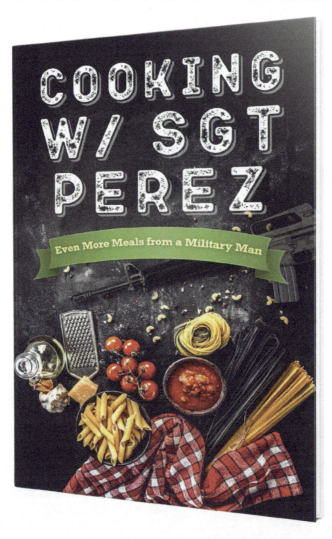

CONTINUING THE JOURNEY OF DELICIOUS AND QUICK CULINARY CREATIONS, "COOKING WITH SGT PEREZ: EVEN MORE MEALS FROM A MILITARY MAN" BRINGS AN ENTIRELY NEW SET OF RECIPES TAILORED FOR THOSE WITH A DYNAMIC LIFESTYLE. IF YOU'VE EVER FELT THE CONSTRAINTS OF A BUSTLING SCHEDULE OR THE DEMANDING NATURE OF TACTICAL PROFESSIONS LIKE THE MILITARY OR LAW ENFORCEMENT, AND YEARN FOR VARIETY AND NUTRITION IN YOUR MEALS, THIS SEQUEL IS CRAFTED JUST FOR YOU. THIS BOOK IS A TESTAMENT TO THE BELIEF THAT EVEN IN THE WHIRLWIND OF OUR DAILY LIVES, PREPARING AND ENJOYING WHOLESOME, TASTY FOOD SHOULD NEVER BE A COMPROMISE.

IN THIS SECOND INSTALLMENT, SGT PEREZ GOES BEYOND THE BASICS, INTRODUCING RECIPES THAT CATER TO A WIDE ARRAY OF DIETARY PREFERENCES AND COOKING METHODS. FROM THE EASE OF CROCKPOT MEALS TO THE FRESHNESS OF VEGETARIAN AND VEGAN DISHES, SMOOTHIE ENTHUSIASTS AND SNACK LOVERS WILL ALSO FIND NEW FAVORITES TO ADD TO THEIR REPERTOIRE.

SHRIMP DIABLO

Diablo, which translates to "devil" in Spanish, alludes to the tomato sauce's hot kick that coats the shrimp.

Ingredients:

- 2 tablespoons Land O Lakes® Butter
- 3 medium (3 cups) zucchini, cut into 1/2-inch slices
- 1 medium (1/2 cup) onion, sliced
- 1 teaspoon finely chopped fresh garlic
- 1 (14.5-ounce) can diced tomatoes with Italian herbs
- 1 (12-ounce) package frozen medium cooked shrimp, thawed, drained
- 1/4 teaspoon ground red pepper (cayenne)
- 2 cups hot cooked rice or couscous

How to Make:

1. Melt butter in 10-inch skillet until sizzling; add zucchini, onion and garlic. Cook over medium-high heat, stirring occasionally, 3-4 minutes or until vegetables are crisply tender.

2. Stir in diced tomatoes, shrimp and red pepper. Continue cooking 3-4 minutes or until mixture comes to a full boil. Reduce heat to medium. Cover: cook, stirring occasionally, 6-8 minutes or until shrimp are heated through. Serve over rice.

BROCCOLI & CHEESE SOUP

Tonight's dinner should be this quick and simple broccoli cheese soup.

Ingredients:

- 1 (14-ounce) can chicken broth
- 1 (12-ounce) package frozen chopped broccoli
- 1 cup Land O Lakes Fat Free Half & Half
- 2 tablespoons all-purpose flour
- 8 (3/4-ounce) slices Land O Lakes® Deli American, quartered

How to Make:

1. Place chicken broth and broccoli in 2-quart saucepan. Cook over medium-high heat 8-10 minutes or until mixture comes to a boil. Reduce heat to medium. Cook 4-6 minutes or until broccoli is tender.
2. Stir together half & half and flour in bowl until smooth. Slowly add flour mixture to soup, stirring constantly. Continue cooking, stirring occasionally, 2-3 minutes or until mixture comes to a full boil. Boil 1 minute. Reduce heat to low. Stir in cheese until melted.

CHICKEN PASTA WITH CIABATTA CROUTONS

The highlight of this dish is the unexpected crunch of the flavored croutons.

Ingredients:

- 2 cups uncooked dried Campanella pasta
- 4 tablespoons Land O Lakes Butter with Olive Oil & Sea Salt
- 2 teaspoons Italian seasoning
- 4 ounces ciabatta bread, cut into 1-inch cubes
- 12 ounces boneless skinless chicken breasts, cut into 1/4-inch-thick strips
- ounces baby broccoli or broccoli florets
- 2 tablespoons fresh lemon juice
- 1 tablespoon finely chopped fresh garlic
- 1/4 teaspoon salt
- 1/4 cup shredded Parmesan cheese, if desired

How to Make:

1. Cook pasta according to package directions. Drain; keep warm.

2. Melt 2 tablespoons Butter with Olive Oil & Sea Salt in 12-inch skillet over medium heat until sizzling. Add Italian seasoning; mix well. Add bread cubes. Cook, stirring occasionally, 3-5 minutes or until bread cubes are slightly crunchy and deep golden brown. Remove bread cubes from skillet.

3. Add chicken to same skillet; cook 4-6 minutes or until lightly browned. Add broccoli and 1 tablespoon lemon juice; continue cooking 8-10 minutes or until broccoli is crisply tender. Remove chicken and broccoli to plate, leaving any sauce in skillet. Cover chicken and broccoli; keep warm.

4. Add remaining 2 tablespoons Butter with Olive Oil & Sea Salt, remaining 1 tablespoon lemon juice, garlic and salt to same skillet. Add pasta; stir to coat pasta with sauce. Stir in bread cubes.

5. Serve cooked chicken and broccoli over pasta. Sprinkle with Parmesan cheese, if desired.

ITALIAN MAC & CHEESE

We've added Italian seasonings to this mac and cheese to give it a unique spin.

Ingredients:

- 8 ounces (2 cups) uncooked penne pasta
- Tablespoons Land O Lakes® Butter
- 1 medium (1/2 cup) onion, chopped
- 2 small zucchinis, halved lengthwise, cut into 1/2-inch chunks
- 3/4 cup sliced roasted red peppers, well drained
- 1/4 cup all-purpose flour
- 1 teaspoon garlic salt
- 1/4 teaspoon pepper
- 2 cups Land O Lakes Half & Half
- 2 teaspoons dried Italian seasoning
- 8-ounce slice Land O Lakes® Provolone Cheese, cubed 1/2 inch
- 1/4 cup Italian-style breadcrumbs

How to Make:

1. Heat oven to 350°f. Spray 3-quart baking dish with no-stick cooking spray; set aside.

2. Cook pasta according to package directions. Drain; keep warm.

3. Meanwhile, melt 4 tablespoons butter in 2-quart heavy saucepan over medium heat until sizzling; add onion. Cook, stirring occasionally, 2-3 minutes or until onion starts to soften. Add zucchini and roasted red peppers; cook 2 minutes. Stir in flour, garlic salt and pepper; continue cooking 1 minute. Gradually stir in half & half and Italian seasoning. Bring to a boil; boil 1 minute. Reduce heat to medium; add cheese. Cook 1-2 minutes or until cheese is melted. Pour mixture over pasta; mix well. Spoon pasta mixture into prepared baking dish.

4. Melt remaining 1 tablespoon butter in 1-quart saucepan. Add breadcrumbs; stir until combined. Sprinkle over pasta mixture. Bake 15-20 minutes or until hot and bubbly and breadcrumbs are browned.

TEXAS COWBOY HASH

Serve this flavorful and filling potato and egg skillet on hectic days when you're short on time.

Ingredients:

- 8 ounces chorizo sausage
- 1 (28-ounce) package frozen diced potatoes with onion and peppers, slightly thawed
- large Land O Lakes Eggs, well beaten
- 2 tablespoons chopped green chiles
- (3/4-ounce) slices Land O Lakes Hot Pepper

How to Make:

1. Cook sausage in 12-inch skillet over medium-heat 6-8 minutes or until no longer pink. Add potatoes; continue cooking, stirring occasionally, 6-8 minutes or until potatoes are tender. Stir in beaten eggs and chiles. Reduce heat to medium. Cook, stirring gently, 1-2 minutes or until eggs are set.
2. Remove from heat, top with cheese slices. Cover: let stand until cheese is melted.
3. Serve with sour cream and salsa, if desired.

BLACKBERRY TEA SMOOTHIE

In this creamy frozen delicacy, use your preferred frozen berries!

Ingredients:

- 3/4 blackberry tea bags
- 1/2 cup boiling water
- 1 cup Land O Lakes® Half & Half
- 1 cup frozen mixed berries (blackberries, blueberries, strawberries and/or raspberries)
- 1 cup raspberry sherbet
- 2 cups ice cubes
- Land O Lakes® Heavy Whipping Cream, whipped
- Fresh berries, if desired
- 2 tablespoons honey

How to Make:

1. Place tea bags in boiling water; let stand 5 minutes. Squeeze tea bags; remove. Cool tea to room temperature.
2. Combine tea and all remaining smoothie ingredients in 5-cup blender container. Cover; process 30-60 seconds or until smooth. Pour into individual glasses. Garnish with whipped cream and fresh berries, if desired.

YOGURT PARFAITS WITH GRANOLA

The parfaits are simple to make, and kids will like them for breakfast or as a nutritious snack.

Ingredients:

- 1/2 cup uncooked old-fashioned or quick-cooking oats
- 1/2 cup coarsely chopped graham crackers
- 3 tablespoons Land O Lakes® Cinnamon Sugar Butter Spread
- 2 cups vanilla yogurt
- 2 cups fresh fruit

How to Make:

1. Heat oven to 350°F.
2. Combine all granola ingredients in bowl; stir well to combine. Spread into lightly greased 9-inch square baking pan. Bake, stirring once, 11-12 minutes or until golden brown. Cool completely; break apart.
3. Layer ingredients starting with 1 tablespoon granola, 1/4 cup yogurt and 1/4 cup fruit; repeat layers ending with granola.
4. Serve immediately or cover each with plastic food wrap. Refrigerate up to 2 hours.

LIME CREAM COOLER

A creamy, cool punch recipe is ideal as a drink at a summer party or as a cool treat on a hot summer day.

Ingredients:

- 1 quart (4 cups) vanilla ice cream, slightly softened
- 1 quart (4 cups) lime sherbet, slightly softened
- 4 cups Land O Lakes® Fat Free Half & Half
- 1 (6-ounce) can froze lemonade concentrate
- 1 (6-ounce) can froze limeade concentrate
- 2 cups water
- 4 cups ginger ale

How to Make:

1. Stir together ice cream, sherbet, and fat free half & half in large punch bowl.
2. Stir together lemonade concentrate, limeade concentrate and water in 1-quart pitcher. Pour over ice cream mixture. Add ginger ale; stir until slightly mixed.

SUMMER SMOOTHIE

This vitamin-rich beverage is made from ripe summer fruits.

Ingredients:

- 1 1/2 cups low fat frozen peach yogurt
- 1 cup chopped fresh cantaloupe
- 1/2 cup fresh raspberries
- 1/2 cup peeled, chopped fresh mango
- 1/4 cup Land O Lakes® Fat Free Half & Half

How to Make:

1. Combine all smoothie ingredients in 5-cup blender container. Cover; blend until smooth.
2. Stir in any one or more stir-ins, if desired. Serve smoothies with spoons.

CHECK OUT

THESE OTHER COOKBOOKS FROM SGT PEREZ

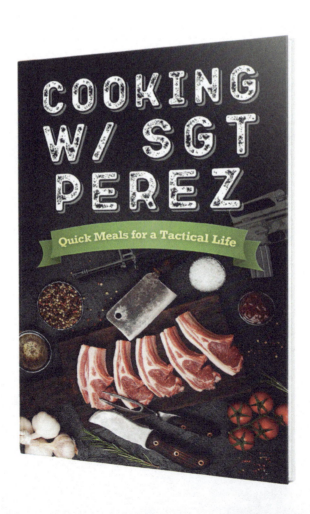

ARE YOU CONSTANTLY ON THE GO? DO YOU LIVE A TACTICAL LIFE THAT DEMANDS A LOT OF YOUR TIME? ARE YOU TIRED OF NOT HAVING DELICIOUS RECIPES TO FUEL YOUR LIFE? ARE YOU LOOKING FOR SOME QUICK, EASY, DELICIOUS, AND HEALTHY RECIPES TO ENJOY DURING YOUR CRAZY LIFE? IF YOU ANSWERED YES TO ANY OF THESE QUESTIONS, YOU ARE GOING TO WANT TO KEEP READING.

IN COOKING WITH SGT PEREZ, YOU WILL FIND LOTS OF RECIPES THAT WILL FUEL YOU AND MAKE YOUR LIFE JUST A BIT SIMPLER. WHETHER YOU ARE CURRENTLY IN A TACTICAL CAREER, LIKE THE MILITARY OR POLICE, OR IF YOU ARE A CIVILIAN THAT LIVES A FAST-PACED LIFE, THESE ARE DELICIOUS RECIPES THAT WILL EASILY FIT INTO YOUR DAY. IF YOU'RE TIRED OF NOT KNOWING WHAT TO FIX FOR DINNER, THEN THIS BOOK IS THE BOOK FOR YOU. TIRED OF FIXING THE SAME THING NIGHT AFTER NIGHT? THIS BOOK CAN GET YOU OUT OF YOUR RUT, AND INTO A DELICIOUS DISH THAT YOU AND YOUR ENTIRE FAMILY WILL ENJOY.

Cinnamony Apple Oatmeal

What You Need:

- Water, 4 c
- Cinnamon, 1 tsp
- Apples, 2
- Old fashioned rolled oatmeal, 2 c

What You Do:

1. Add everything to your cooker, but don't stir them together.
2. Cover, and let it cook on low for eight to nine hours.
3. Once done, stir everything together and enjoy.

Apple Oatmeal

What You Need:

- Fat-free vanilla yogurt, 4 tbsp
- Chopped walnuts, .25 c
- Raisins, .25 c
- Maple syrup, .25 c
- Chopped apple, .5 c
- Rolled oats, 1.5 c
- Cinnamon, .5 tsp
- Unsweetened apple juice, 3 c

What You Do:

1. Mix all of the ingredients together in your slow cooker.
2. Cover, and set to cook for eight to nine hours on low.
3. Once you are ready to eat, stir everything together and enjoy.

Texas Omelet Wrap

What You Need:

- Salsa, 1 tbsp – optional
- Shredded cheddar cheese, 2 tbsp
- Whole-wheat wrap
- Black bean dip, 2 tbsp
- Chopped scallions, 1 tbsp
- Pepper
- Hot sauce, .5 tsp
- Egg white
- Egg

What You Do:

1. Grease your slow cooker with some cooking spray.
2. Beat together the egg, egg white, hot sauce, pepper, scallions, and cheese.
3. Pour the eggs into your slow cooker and cover. Set to high for two to three hours.
4. In the last few minutes of the cooking time, heat the wrap for a few seconds in the microwave and spread the black bean dip across it. If your dip is cold, microwave it for a few seconds to make it spreadable.
5. Once the omelet is set, remove from the cooker and lay it on the wrap. You may have to slice it into pieces to fit, depending on the shape of your cooker.
6. Add on some salsa if you want. Roll up the wrap and enjoy.

Breakfast Casserole

What You Need:

- Pepper, .5 tsp
- Salt, .5 tsp
- Milk, .75 c
- Eggs, 8
- Reduced-fat shredded cheddar, .75 c
- Cooked turkey breakfast sausage, .5 lb
- Frozen hash browns, 16 oz

What You Do:

1. If it's not cooked already, brown up the sausage and drain off the grease.

2. Grease your slow cooker with some cooking spray.

3. Lay a third of the potatoes in the bottom of the cooker. Top with a third of the sausage and a third of the cheese. Repeat this two more times.

4. Beat the pepper, salt, milk, and eggs together. Pour this over the potatoes and sausage.

5. Cover, and set to cook for four to five hours on low or until the edges are browned, and the middle is set.

6. Slice into six wedges and enjoy.

Southwest Breakfast Casserole

What You Need:

- Cayenne pepper, .25 tsp
- Seasoned salt, 1 tsp
- Fat-free evaporated milk, 12 oz can
- Eggs, 8
- Chopped cilantro 3 tbsp
- Reduced-fat shredded Mexican cheese blend, 1.5 c
- Corn kernels, 1 c
- Shredded hash brown, 4 c
- Finely chopped onion, .5 c
- Chopped red bell pepper
- Drained and rinsed black beans, 14 oz can

What You Do:

1. Start by greasing your slow cooker with some cooking spray.
2. Mix together the cilantro, cheese, corn, potatoes, onion, bell pepper, and black beans and then dump everything into the cooker.
3. Beat together the cayenne, salt, milk, and eggs. Pour over the potato mixture.
4. Cover and allow the casserole to refrigerate for at least four hours.
5. Once you are ready to cook, place the slow cooker insert into the cooker base. Cover, and set to cook for three to five hours on low. The eggs should be set and edges browned.
6. Uncover and turn the cooker off. Allow the casserole to sit for 15 minutes before slicing into eight wedges.
7. Serve and enjoy.

Breakfast Barley and Fruit

What You Need:

- Chopped walnuts, 2 tbsp
- Allspice, .5 tsp
- Chopped apple
- Chopped dates, .25 c
- Chopped dried apricots, .25 c
- Dried cranberries, .25 c
- Pearl barley, .66 c
- Orange juice 1 c
- Water, 1.66 c

What You Do:

1. Grease your slow cooker with some nonstick spray.

2. Add the allspice, apple, dates, apricots, cranberries, barley, water, and orange juice to your cooker and stir everything together.

3. Cover and set to cook for six to eight hours on the lowest setting, or until the liquid has been absorbed by the barley and it's tender. It may look thin at first, but it will thicken as it cools.

4. Serve.

Gingerbread Waffles

What You Need:

- Coconut sugar, 4 tbsp
- Ground ginger, 2 tsp
- Cinnamon, 1.5 tsp
- Salt, .25 tsp
- Baking soda, .25 tsp
- Ground flax seeds, 1 tbsp
- Spelt flour, 1 c
- Baking powder, 2 tsp
- Olive oil, 1.5 tbsp
- Molasses, 2 tbsp
- Apple cider vinegar, 1 tbsp
- Coconut milk, 1 c

What You Do:

1. Preheat and grease your waffle iron.
2. You can also make these as pancakes if you don't have a waffle iron.
3. Mix the dry ingredients together. Stir together the wet ingredients. Now, mix everything together until just combined. It should be about the consistency of cake batter. If it's too thick, add a little more milk.
4. Once the waffle iron is hot, pour in the batter and let them cook according to your device's instructions.
5. Remove the waffles and continue with the rest of the batter. Enjoy.

Breakfast Sandwich

What You Need:

- "Pepper
- Pickle, 6 slices
- Sliced tomatoes, 2
- Greens, 1 c
- Vegan mayo, 2 tbsp
- Bread, 6 slices
- Melty vegan cheese, 3 slices
- Salt, .5 tsp
- Garlic powder, .5 tsp
- Turmeric, 1 tsp
- Extra firm tofu, 14 oz – pressed and sliced in the 6 slices
- Coconut oil, 1 tbsp"

What You Do:

1. Season one side of each tofu slice with turmeric, pepper, garlic, and salt. The other side gets seasoned later.

2. Heat the oil in a skillet and place the tofu seasoned side down in the pan. Season the other side now. Let cook for about three minutes until crispy. Flip and fry for another three minutes.

3. Lay two slices of tofu side by side on a baking sheet and top with a piece of cheese. Broil for three minutes, or until the cheese melts.

4. Spread the mayo on the bread and add on the tofu, greens, tomatoes, and pickles. Enjoy.

Tofu Breakfast of Champions

What You Need:

- Spice Mix:
- Garlic powder, .25 tsp
- Turmeric, .75 tsp
- Salt, 1 tsp
- Cumin, 1 tsp
- Chili powder, 1 tsp
- Nutritional yeast, 2 tbsp
- Tofu:
- Rinsed black beans, 19 oz
- Large block of tofu
- Minced garlic, 2 cloves
- Chopped onion, .5
- Chopped red pepper
- Sliced button mushrooms, 8 oz
- Oil, 1 tbsp

What You Do:

1. Mix the spice mixture together and set aside.
2. Get the oil good and hot in a pan. Once hot, place in the garlic, onion, pepper, and mushrooms, cooking for about eight minutes or until it starts to brown.
3. Break up the tofu and add it into the skillet. Mash around until it looks like scrambled eggs. Mix in the beans and the spice mixture. Cook for about five to eight minutes and enjoy.

Breakfast Casserole

What You Need:

- Green onions
- Cherry tomatoes
- Chives
- Vegan cheese for topping
- Liquid smoke, .5 tsp – optional
- Turmeric, 1 tsp
- Soy sauce, 1 tsp
- Paprika, 2.5 tsp - divided
- BBQ sauce, 1 tbsp
- Tempeh, 5 oz
- Vegan cheese, .5 c
- Chopped chives, 1 tbsp
- Cornstarch, 1 tbsp
- Salt
- Olive oil, 1.5 tbsp
- Silken tofu, 10 oz
- Pepper
- Chopped onion
- Diced potatoes, 5

What You Do:

1. Start by boiling the potatoes until soft.
2. Get the oil good and hot in a pan and then cook half of the onions until they become translucent. Mix in the potatoes, pepper, salt, and a teaspoon of paprika. This should continue cooking for about five minutes so that they are crispy and brown. Set to the side.
3. As the potatoes boil, get the "bacon" ready. Slice the tempeh into small cubes. Add oil to the skillet and add the tempeh along with the BBQ sauce, liquid smoke, soy sauce, half of the onions, and a teaspoon of paprika. Add some pepper and salt and cook for five minutes.
4. Mix together the salt, remaining paprika, turmeric, cornstarch, oil, and the tofu in a bowl. Mix until they become smooth. Mix in the chives and cheese.
5. Turn the oven to 350.
6. Add the potatoes and tempeh into a baking dish and then add in the tofu mixture. Top with some extra cheese and bake 15 to 20 minutes.
7. Serve with tomatoes, parsley, and chives.

Scrambled Eggs with Peppers and Onions

What You Need:

- Pepper and salt
- Cilantro, 1 tbsp
- Scallion
- Red bell pepper, .5
- Olive oil, 2 tbsp
- Eggs, 3
- Hot sauce - optional

What You Do:

1. Begin by cracking the eggs into a small bowl and sprinkle in some pepper and salt to taste. Whisk the eggs together until they become uniform in color.

2. Add the oil to a skillet and let it warm. As the pan heats up, dice up the ½ of a red bell pepper and the scallion. Once heated, add the pepper to the pan and cook it for three to four minutes. You can sprinkle some pepper to season the bell pepper if you would like.

3. Pour the eggs into the skillet over the peppers. Allow the eggs to sit for a little while to set up on the bottom, and then scramble them, making sure that you scrape down the sides from time to time.

4. Once the eggs are just about cooked through, add in the scallions and finish cooking. Top with some cilantro and hot sauce if you would like.

Egg Muffins

What You Need:

- Muffin tin liners
- Pepper and salt
- Diced mushrooms, .5 c
- Diced roasted red peppers, .5 c
- Chopped spinach, 2 c
- Eggs, 12
- Pre-cooked organic turkey sausage, 4 pieces

What You Do:

1. Start by setting your oven to 350. Line a cupcake tin with the liners and set to the side.

2. In a bowl, add all of the eggs and beat them together. Add all of the other ingredients and mix them together. Season with some pepper and salt.

3. Divide the egg mixture between the muffin cups and then bake them for 18 to 20 minutes, or until the eggs are set. Enjoy two muffins along with some approved fruit.

DO YOU LOVE

FANTASY FICTION?

CHECK OUT N. ALESSANDRO PENINTON'S NEWEST BOOK "THE ROSE IN THE GLASS DOME"

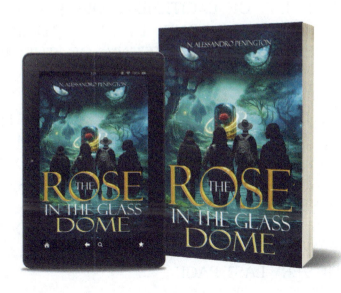

EMBARK ON A SPELLBINDING JOURNEY THROUGH THE VEILS OF DARKNESS!

PREPARE TO BE SWEPT AWAY INTO A WORLD WHERE MAGIC HOLDS SWAY AND DANGER LURKS AT EVERY SHADOWED CORNER. "THE ROSE IN THE GLASS DOME" BECKONS YOU INTO A REALM WHERE THE LINE BETWEEN REALITY AND NIGHTMARE BLURS, AND ONLY COURAGE AND CUNNING CAN CARVE A PATH TO SALVATION.

IN THE HEART OF THIS MESMERIZING TALE, A QUARTET OF INTREPID SOULS VENTURES FORTH ON A MISSION SHROUDED IN PERIL. THEIR QUEST? TO RESCUE ROSE FROM THE CLUTCHES OF A MONSTROUS TERROR. YET, FATE WEAVES A TANGLED WEB, ENSNARING THEM IN A CONSPIRACY THAT THREATENS TO PLUNGE THE ENTIRE KINGDOM INTO MADNESS.

BRIMMING WITH PULSE-POUNDING SUSPENSE AND SPINE-CHILLING TWISTS, THIS EPIC ADVENTURE IS A MASTERFUL FUSION OF ENCHANTMENT AND PERIL. FEEL THE PULSE OF EXCITEMENT QUICKEN AS YOU JOURNEY ALONGSIDE OUR HEROES, THEIR FATE INTERTWINED WITH THE DESTINY OF THE REALM ITSELF.

"THE ROSE IN THE GLASS DOME" IS A TOUR DE FORCE, BLENDING THE ALLURE OF MYSTICAL REALMS WITH THE GRITTY DETERMINATION OF THOSE WHO DARE TO DEFY DARKNESS. ARE YOU READY TO HEED THE CALL AND IMMERSE YOURSELF IN A SAGA WHERE BRAVERY KNOWS NO BOUNDS? JOIN US, AND BRACE YOURSELF FOR AN ODYSSEY THAT WILL LEAVE YOU SPELLBOUND UNTIL THE VERY LAST PAGE.

GET YOUR

COPY TODAY

ON AMAZON

Made in the USA
Monee, IL
04 December 2024

72297391R00046